WOMEN WHO DARE

Margaret Mead

BY AIMEE HESS

Pomegranate
SAN FRANCISCO

LIBRARY OF CONGRESS
WASHINGTON, DC

Published by Pomegranate Communications, Inc.
Box 808022, Petaluma CA 94975
800 227 1428; www.pomegranate.com

Pomegranate Europe Ltd.
Unit 1, Heathcote Business Centre, Hurlbutt Road
Warwick, Warwickshire CV34 6TD, UK
[+44] 0 1926 430111; sales@pomeurope.co.uk

Amy Pastan, Series Editor

In association with the Library of Congress, Pomegranate publishes other books in the Women Who
Dare® series, as well as calendars, books of postcards, posters, and Knowledge Cards® featuring
daring women. Please contact the publisher for more information.

Library of Congress Cataloging-in-Publication Data

Hess, Aimee.
    Women who dare : Margaret Mead / by Aimee Hess.
        p. cm. — (Women who dare)
    Includes bibliographical references.
    ISBN-13: 978-0-7649-3875-7
    1. Mead, Margaret, 1901–1978. 2. Women anthropologists—United States—Biography.
    3. Ethnology—Melanesia—Field work. 4. Melanesia—Social life and customs.   I. Title.

    GN21.M43H47 2007
    301.092—dc22
    [B]

                                    2006050343

Pomegranate Catalog No. A132
Designed by Harrah Lord, Yellow House Studio, Rockport, ME
Printed in Korea

16 15 14 13 12 11 10 09 08 07   10 9 8 7 6 5 4 3 2 1

**All photographs are courtesy of the Institute for Intercultural Studies, Inc., New York,
unless indicated otherwise. See photo captions for photographers and additional credits.**

FRONT COVER: *Mead in native dress flanked by two Samoan girls, c. 1926*
BACK COVER: *Mead and Gregory Bateson working in mosquito room, Tambunam, 1938*
        PHOTOGRAPH BY GREGORY BATESON

PREFACE

FOR TWO HUNDRED YEARS, the Library of Congress, the oldest national cultural institution in the United States, has been gathering materials necessary to tell the stories of women in America. The last third of the twentieth century witnessed a great surge of popular and scholarly interest in women's studies and women's history that has led to an outpouring of works in many formats. Drawing on women's history resources in the collections of the Library of Congress, the Women Who Dare book series is designed to provide readers with an entertaining introduction to the life of a notable American woman or a significant topic in women's history.

From its beginnings in 1800 as a legislative library, the Library of Congress has grown into a national library that houses both a universal collection of knowledge and the mint record of American creativity. Congress' decision to purchase Thomas Jefferson's personal library to replace the books and maps burned during the British occupation in 1814 set the Congressional Library on the path of collecting with the breadth of Jefferson's interests. Not just American imprints were to be acquired, but foreign-language materials as well, and Jefferson's library already included works by American and European women.

The Library of Congress has some 121 million items, largely housed in closed stacks in three buildings on Capitol Hill that contain twenty public reading rooms. The incredible, wide-ranging collections include books, maps, prints, newspapers, broadsides, diaries, letters, posters, musical scores, photographs, audio and video recordings, and documents available only in digital formats. The Library serves first-time users and the most experienced researchers alike.

I hope that you, the reader, will seek and find in the pages of this book information that will further your understanding of women's history. In addition, I hope you will continue to explore the topic of this book in a library near you, in person at the Library of Congress, or by visiting the Library on the World Wide Web at http://www.loc.gov. Happy reading!

—JAMES H. BILLINGTON, The Librarian of Congress

I went to Samoa to find out more about human beings, human beings like ourselves in everything except their culture. Through the accidents of history, these cultures had developed so differently from ours that knowledge of them could shed a kind of light upon us, upon our potentialities and our limitations, that was unique.

—Margaret Mead

O n a late summer day in 1925, twenty-three-year-old Margaret Mead, standing just five feet three inches tall and weighing under a hundred pounds, boarded a train in Philadelphia on her way across the country to San Francisco. From there, she would fly to Hawaii, and then on to her final destination, the remote island of Samoa, nine thousand miles away, where she would live in a room separated from her inquiring neighbors only by screens. A graduate student in the emerging field of anthropology, Mead had spent her summer "getting inoculations and frantically assembling my field equipment—spare glasses, cotton dresses, a camera, pencils, and notebooks." With virtually no practical training, she planned to spend nine months studying a culture worlds apart from her own, before it "disappeared forever."

Mead, who had never before been on a ship or stayed in a hotel, left with "all the courage of complete ignorance." But she had never been one to be unsure of herself. As she walked away from her family and young husband, her father claimed, "She never looked back!"

■ *Margaret Mead, self-portrait, pastel on paper, c. 1914–1915. "By the age of ten,"*
Mead once told a friend, "I was a very sober little lady."

LEARNING TO OBSERVE THE WORLD

THE FIRST BABY born at West Park Hospital in Philadelphia, on December 16, 1901, Margaret Mead was the oldest daughter of Edward Sherwood Mead and Emily Fogg Mead. Both social scientists, the Meads were progressive thinkers. "In some ways my upbringing was well ahead of my time," Mead would later write. "Mother's advanced ideas, the way in which all children in our home were treated as persons, the kinds of books I read . . . represented an extraordinary sophistication and a view of children that was rare in my childhood."

As a result of her parents' scholarly pursuits, Mead often changed houses several times a year throughout her childhood, usually settling in small, academic towns. The frequent moves gave Mead a unique perspective on the concept of home. "For me," she wrote in her autobiography *Blackberry Winter,* "moving and staying at home, traveling and arriving, are all of a piece."

■ *Mead as a baby, 1902. Mead's father nicknamed her "Punk," calling her younger brother, Richard, the "boy-punk." Mead called this "a reversal of the usual pattern, according to which the girl is only a female version of the true human being, the boy."*

Mead's birth was followed by that of her brother, Richard, in 1903. The next child was a girl whom Mead, now six, was allowed to name; she chose the name Katherine, but the baby died at nine months. Two more sisters, Elizabeth and Priscilla, arrived in 1909 and 1911. Mead's paternal grandmother, Martha Ramsay Meade, rounded out the household.

■ *Edward Sherwood Mead (middle) with children Margaret and Richard, c. 1909–1910.*
Edward Sherwood Mead was an economist and professor at the Wharton School.
His work took his family all over Pennsylvania, where he set up satellite
campuses and established a night school for working students.

A progressive thinker like her son and daughter-in-law, Martha Ramsay Meade was an important influence on Mead's childhood. Other than two years of kindergarten and half-day attendance during the fourth grade, Mead was home-schooled until high school by her grandmother, a former teacher, who believed that children should not be made to sit still for more than an hour at a time. As a result, Mead remembered, "I learned to observe the world around me and to note what I saw." In addition, Mead's mother enlisted the teachings of craftsmen for her children to learn skills, such as basketry, carpentry, and painting, providing a

■ *Margaret and brother Richard, Nantucket, Massachusetts, summer 1911. "Margaret and Richard were expected to do everything together," Mead wrote, adding "Our life together was placid and unexciting."*

well-rounded and varied education, an experience not many children of her generation shared.

Mead attended regular high school in Doylestown, Pennsylvania. Shortly before she was to leave for her chosen college, Wellesley, her father suffered major financial losses, and Mead instead attended the less expensive DePauw University in Indiana, her father's alma mater. DePauw was a huge disappointment for Mead, who was rejected by most of the other girls for her strange way of dressing, individualist attitude, and eastern accent: "I was confronted, for the first time in my life, with being thoroughly unacceptable to almost everyone and on grounds in which I had previously been taught to take pride." More importantly, she did not find "brilliant students, students who would challenge me to stretch my mind" as she had hoped. At the end of the school year, in 1920, Mead transferred to Barnard College, the female branch of Columbia University in New York, where she would be in the same city as her fiancé, Luther Cressman.

■ *Martha Ramsay Meade, 1918. Martha Ramsay Meade spelled her last name with a final "e," a letter the Mead family eventually dropped. Margaret Mead's closeness to her grandmother sparked a lifelong interest in relationships between grandparents and grandchildren. She devoted two chapters in her autobiography to the subject—the first "On Being a Granddaughter," and later, "On Being a Grandmother," in which she wrote, "In the presence of grandparent and grandchild, past and future merge in the present."* LCMS-32441-114

■ *Diary,* (right) *Emily Fogg Mead, "Characteristics at 6 Years," c. January 1908.*

■ *Diary,* (below) *Margaret Mead, record of sister Elizabeth's language development, c. 1911–1912. Mead's mother devotedly took notes of the experiences and characteristics of her first daughter's early childhood, eventually filling thirteen volumes. As Mead grew older, she assumed this responsibility for her younger siblings. Later she wrote, "I learned to make these notes with love, carrying on what Mother had begun."*

Priscilla wants
some food.

I thought mother
up dried floor.

Get out of my
way

Mae no rock me I rock
dolly, dolly comes first.

I feed my dolly, my
dolly hungry

I had button hook
yesterday

I wipe my nose,
my nose running.

Characteristics at 6 years

Marriage and Mentors

MEAD HAD MET Cressman in high school, when his older brother, a Doylestown teacher, brought him to dinner at the Mead house. She kept in touch with Cressman, a classics scholar in his third year of college study, and the couple got engaged the following winter. Mead would not marry Cressman, however, until after college. She wanted to get the most out of her studies, and at Barnard, she immediately felt at home. She fell into a close group of friends who called themselves the Ash Can Cats, and joined the debate squad. More informal debates were known to go on late into the night at the apartment she shared with fellow students, although Mead characteristically retired early.

■ *Luther Cressman and Margaret Mead, c. 1917–1918. Mead described Cressman as having "an engaging grin and a wry sense of humor, yet he took life seriously and, like my mother, was willing to see life whole." Cressman was interested in following his uncle, a Lutheran minister, into the clergy. At that time, Mead said, "a minister's wife was what I wanted to be," and Cressman fit the bill perfectly, especially after Mead encouraged him to switch to the Episcopal faith, the religion she had chosen for herself at age eleven.*

■ *Mead with fellow Ash Can Cats Léonie Adams (left) and Eleanor Pelham Kortheuer (right), c. 1920. The group of friends got their name from a drama teacher who once said, "You girls sit up all night readin' po'try, 'n come to class lookin' like ash can cats."*

At Barnard, Mead studied psychology and literature. Still searching for a field in which she could make a difference, she took a course in anthropology, the study of culture and social customs. There, she met a graduate student named Ruth Benedict, who would become her mentor and lifelong friend. The field of anthropology, just emerging in the academic world, had only one full-time faculty member in the department at that time: Benedict's mentor Franz Boas, or "Papa Franz," as many of his female students—among them writer Zora Neale Hurston—called him.

Boas stressed the importance of recording preliterate societies before they disappeared. Mead was immediately attracted to anthropology as a field that needed fresh young scholars vigorous enough to take on fieldwork under tough conditions. Benedict explained to her,

■ *Ruth Benedict, c. 1920s. Fifteen years Mead's senior, Benedict was a graduate student and new to anthropology when she and Mead met, but she would later become an anthropologist of much renown. Close friends until Benedict's death in 1968, Mead and Benedict were rumored to be lovers as well, a relationship Mead's daughter confirms in her autobiography.*

■ *Often called the "father of American anthropology," the German-born Franz Boas pioneered the idea of cultural relativism, believing that each race is biologically equal and differences are a result of culture or nurture, not nature. He felt that each culture should be studied separately by living among the people and participating in their daily lives, rather than by viewing them through the eyes of another culture. In this manner, Boas believed it would be possible to come to an absolute truth about the way culture affects civilization.*

"Professor Boas and I have nothing to offer but an opportunity to do work that matters." In this new field of anthropology, Mead would make a name for herself. She determined to get her master's in psychology as she had originally planned, but to pursue a doctorate in anthropology.

Mead also determined to marry, despite an offer from her father of "a trip around the world and a very liberal allowance" if she gave up that plan. The marriage, however, went forward in 1923, in a small Episcopal ceremony back home in Pennsylvania.

As a doctoral candidate, Mead was eager to get out of the university and into the field. Boas encouraged her to consider Polynesia, a region she had already significantly studied. He also suggested a possible research topic: adolescence. Boas was interested in whether adolescence was as difficult for youths of other cultures as it was for American teens. Most Americans felt that adolescence was turbulent because of puberty and natural changes, both unavoidable factors. But if Mead could provide evidence showing otherwise, the ramifications would be tremendous, suggesting that the difficulty of adolescence in the United States is a result of American culture rather than biology.

Mead settled on American Samoa, where boats came through every three weeks. The rear admiral in charge of the naval base there was a friend of Cressman's father, and could provide a friendly contact should Mead need anything. Her father agreed to pay her way there and back, and Mead secured a fellowship with a stipend of $150 a month to support herself while she was there. Her husband, by then pursuing a doctorate in sociology, also received a fellowship to study in Europe; the two planned to meet again in Europe after a year apart.

COMING OF AGE IN SAMOA

Mead left her family in Philadelphia and headed to Samoa by way of San Francisco and Hawaii. She reached Pago Pago, one of the larger cities in American Samoa, on the last day of August in 1925. Stuck there for six weeks while she waited for her stipend to arrive by boat, Mead stayed in a ramshackle hotel and studied the language she would have to master before she could begin her fieldwork. For one hour a day she worked under the tutelage of a Samoan nurse, and for seven additional hours, she crammed vocabulary. She also studied the geography of the area and chose a location for her fieldwork: the island of Ta'u, home to a cluster of four villages all within walking distance of one another, one hundred miles east of Pago Pago. There, she settled with a Navy man and his family, the only white household in the area, from whence she could "be in and out of the native homes from early in the morning until late at night and still have a bed to sleep on and wholesome food." She also confided to Ruth Benedict that "there would be no place to work in a native house—and no privacy for work. Every word I wrote they'd be looking over my shoulder."

Mead stayed in Samoa for a total of nine months. Every six weeks, a boat dropped off letters for her and picked up mail to send home. These letters—the only contact she had with loved ones—contained news and professional advice from Boas and Benedict, and they sustained her through a lonely and difficult time. Her research, however, was worth it. She discovered the Samoans' attitude toward sex to be much freer than in America. These less-conservative views allowed

■ *Margaret Mead's room in Samoa, c. 1925–1926.* "My room is half of the back porch of the dispensary quarters buildings," she wrote home in a letter on November 14, 1925. "There is a loosely woven bamboo screen which divides my room from the porch outside the dispensary and here the Samoan children gather to peek through the holes and display their few English words or chatter endlessly in Samoan."

■ *Mead in native dress flanked by two Samoan girls, c. 1926.* As a woman, Mead was able to collect information about women that a man could not. It also helped that she did not look much older than her adolescent subjects.

adolescents the freedom to experiment sexually, and she concluded that the lack of sexual restrictions made Samoan adolescence smoother than the awkward and often unhappy adolescence of American children.

Mead left Samoa in June 1926, eager to share her research. She boarded the SS *Chitral* in Sydney, headed to meet Cressman in Marseilles. A strikingly handsome fellow passenger made the voyage more exciting than Mead had expected.

Reo Fortune, a young scholar from New Zealand, was as starved for stimulating company aboard the ship as Mead. The two spent almost the entire seven-week trip talking, sharing thoughts both academic and personal, and, as Mead later wrote, "falling in love."

In Marseilles, Cressman waited eagerly for his young wife, whom he had not seen in almost a year, to disembark from the ship. He waited a long time; Mead and Fortune were in such intense conversation that they did not notice the boat had docked, and she was the last passenger off the ship. She wrote later, "That is one of the moments I would take back and live differently, if I could. There are not many such moments, but that is one of them."

Not one to hide things, Mead told Cressman about Fortune right away. Cressman took the news calmly and gave Mead the opportunity to decide her own path with no pressure from him. Unsure, Mead moved back to New York with her husband, started a job at the American Museum of Natural History in New York City, and worked diligently on summing up her findings from Samoa in two works: the more scholarly *Social Organization of Manu'a* (1930), and the general-audience-friendly *Coming of Age in Samoa* (1928).

■ *Numerous articles were written about Mead's experiences among other cultures. This one offers a somewhat romanticized view of her stay in Samoa.*

LOVE AND WORK

TWO YEARS passed before Mead finally decided to leave Cressman, who later wrote, "Our parting in 1928 was without bitterness but not without hurt." Aiding her decision was the discovery that a tipped uterus would prevent her from bringing a child to term without miscarrying. Cressman, too, was going through a crisis of faith and ultimately decided to leave the ministry. "I had married Luther with the hope of rearing a houseful of children in a country parish," Mead explained. Now that both of these circumstances were out of the question, she "decided to choose a life of shared field work and intellectual endeavor." In Fortune, Mead would have a partner in the field and would not again have to confront the loneliness she had endured in Samoa.

She obtained a quick divorce in Mexico and lost no time in arranging a leave of absence from the museum and planning fieldwork with Fortune. For this they chose the Admiralty Islands in New Guinea, where Mead planned to study primitive children, and Fortune, religion and ancestors. After marrying in Auckland, the couple made their way to New Guinea, settling into a small village named Pere on the island of Manus. Mead called Manus a "primitive Venice"; the houses sat above water on stilts, and villagers traveled primarily by canoe.

■ *Mead and Reo Fortune, Pere Village, Manus, Admiralty Islands, 1928. In Manus, work went smoothly for the newlyweds; Mead remembered that time together as "the best field trip we ever had."*
PHOTOGRAPH BY REO FORTUNE OR MARGARET MEAD

Mead, whom the local people called "Piyap," or Woman of the West, brought paper for the children to draw on so she could see how they related to reality; she eventually collected thirty-five thousand drawings. Although Mead had malaria most of the time she was there and had to use crutches due to a fractured ankle, she was still able to accomplish a significant amount of research.

■ *Mead and Manus children on a canoe, 1928. "Children of three or four can pole canoes ten times their size, handling a pole ten feet high," she wrote in a December 16, 1928, letter home.*
PHOTOGRAPH BY REO FORTUNE

■ Catching Fish in a Net, *pencil drawing by Kilipak, age thirteen, Manus, 1928. During her research in Manus, Mead found that the way children use animism in their drawings varies depending on the beliefs and values of adults in that culture.*

■ *Margaret Mead on crutches, Pere Village, Manus, 1929. While doing fieldwork in Manus, Mead fell and broke her ankle, already weak from a previous break in 1924. The Manus people made her crutches out of canoe poles and wooden pillows.*

PHOTOGRAPH BY
REO FORTUNE

Returning to New York in 1929, Mead learned that her book *Coming of Age in Samoa* was selling well and had already made her somewhat of a popular name. She settled back into her work at the museum, and both she and Fortune worked feverishly for a few years before gearing up for more fieldwork.

After a brief and discouraging stint studying Native Americans in Omaha, Mead and Fortune planned to return to New Guinea. Mead insisted on postponing the trip long enough for her to write "Kinship in the Admiralty Islands," in response to an anthropology student who had criticized her for not fully understanding the kinship system of Manus. Mead later wrote, "This so angered me that I decided to postpone our field trip until I had written 'Kinship in the Admiralty Islands,' which was the most detailed monograph on kinship published up to that time."

In September 1931, the husband-and-wife anthropology team again trekked halfway across the world with little knowledge of exactly where they would end up. Mead's intention was to study sex roles in several different cultures. When they arrived in New Guinea, they enlisted the help of porters to carry their six months' worth of supplies. The porters' load included Mead, slung in a hammock between two sticks, because a weak ankle prevented her from completing the climb over the mountains, "sometimes up almost perpendicular cliffs and sometimes in riverbeds." The ride, she later reported, made her feel "a little sea-sickish." When they got to the remote region of Alitoa, only halfway to their destination, the porters refused to go any further. Mead and Fortune were stuck among a simple people they called the Arapesh. For six months, the pair did their best to research in what they felt was not an ideal cultural setting.

■ *Mundugumor paintings, December 4, 1932. Left: Lizard and frog by Maikava, seventeen-year-old male. Right: Painting by Yeshimba, adult male. After her success in collecting children's drawings in Manus, Mead continued to use drawing as a method to learn about the ways people of certain cultures relate to reality.*

Mead found the Arapesh quite peaceful, but Fortune found them just the opposite and even wrote a scholarly piece titled "Arapesh Warfare." This difference of professional opinion may have presaged the dissolution of their union. Fortune no longer treated Mead's bouts of malaria tenderly, but expected her to tough them out like he would: "His way of treating illness in himself was to go out and climb a mountain, however raging his fever, in order to fight the sickness out of his system." Fortune also mandated a strict separation between their work, which Mead felt took a toll on the work's validity, a factor she would not tolerate.

After nine months, Mead and Fortune found a ride up the Sepik River and settled among a new community, the Mundugumor people. "The natives are superficially agreeable," Mead wrote at the time, "but . . . they go in for cannibalism, headhunting, infanticide, incest, avoidance and joking relationships, and biting lice in half with their teeth." After two and a half months among the Mundugumor, Mead's relationship with Fortune had become strained, to say the least. Disheartened and bedraggled, they made their way up the Sepik to join a group at the main government station for Christmas 1932. There, they would run into an old Cambridge classmate of Fortune's, Gregory Bateson.

"You're tired," Gregory Bateson said to Margaret Mead at their first meeting. His concern was a far cry from Fortune's increasingly harsh attitude toward her health. Mead and Fortune were both happy to exchange notes with a fellow scholar, and Bateson, who had been doing fieldwork among the Iatmul, was happy to have companionship. The threesome decided to stay close enough together that they could continue to converse on a regular basis. Fortune and Mead settled on Tchambuli Lake, and Bateson settled nearby. They hired someone to bring messages back and forth several times a day, and visited each other regularly, an arrangement made slightly awkward by the obvious chemistry between Mead and Bateson.

■ *Gregory Bateson, Mead, and Reo Fortune, July 1933. The three anthropologists had just arrived in Sydney together after completing fieldwork in New Guinea, a trip in which Mead's marriage to Fortune deteriorated and her relationship with Bateson—whom she would marry in 1936—began.*

After four months among the Tchambuli, the odd triangle went their separate ways. Mead returned to New York and began work on her next book, *Sex and Temperament in Three Primitive Societies*. She based the book—which one reviewer called "among the most thoroughly entertaining works in any genre to be published in a long, long time"—on her research into gender roles, concluding that sex roles are man-made rather than biological and that gender discrimination is based on cultural dictations.

Now estranged from Fortune, Mead did not lose touch with Bateson; in fact, they wrote passionate letters back and forth, reuniting in Ireland for a trip in the summer of 1934. That same year, a social scientist named Larry Frank organized a monthlong interdisciplinary conference in Hanover, New Hampshire, which led to a widening of Mead's interest in uniting the social sciences.

Watching the way the Mundugumor treated their children—unwanted babies were often thrown in the river to die—Mead had decided she wanted to have a child no matter how many miscarriages it took. From the beginning, she had not thought Fortune father material. Certainly this was on her mind as her marriage to Fortune fell apart and she and Bateson fell in love. Mead divorced Fortune in 1935.

Soon after her second divorce, Mead and Bateson were married and chose to study the cultural aspects of schizophrenia in Bali. A talented photographer, Bateson planned on taking about 2,500 pictures in Bali. Instead, he took ten times that many and used 22,000 feet of 16 mm film. He and Mead bought processing equipment and set up a film lab so they could process up to 1,600 pictures in one night. They also set about making a film, *Trance and Dance in Bali,* which would become an ethnographic classic.

■ *Mead and I Madé Kalér interviewing subjects, Bajoeng Gedé, Bali, c. 1937. Mead was delighted with I Madé Kalér's dedication and skill as a secretary: "He takes synchronized notes on ceremonies, keeps calendrical records of coming events . . . makes Dutch, Malay, or Balinese translations of anything he is given, turns his mother into an informant when he goes home for a holiday, takes his bath in an icy stream three miles away at 6 A.M. so as to always be on hand . . . and takes down conversations as ungrammatically and brokenly as they occur."* PHOTOGRAPH BY GREGORY BATESON

The couple remained in Bali for two years. The scattered news they received from Europe told them that a war was coming, but before they returned home, they needed to do additional fieldwork in a fresh location to compare the new techniques they had been developing. No other anthropologist had ever used photographs as such an integral part of his or her methods, and Mead and Bateson were eager to show the validity of these field techniques by using them on another culture.

They decided to return to New Guinea and study the Tambunam people, an Iatmul tribe similar to ones Bateson had already studied. His knowledge of their language and customs would make the fieldwork go more smoothly.

■ *Mead and Bateson working in mosquito room, Tambunam, 1938. "When the lamps are lit inside our cage, we can't see out and forget that we ourselves are simply washed in light," Mead wrote, a circumstance that made her feel as if she were living "comfortably in a show window and at the same time keep[ing] up continuous observations of the crowd that gathers outside."*
PHOTOGRAPH BY GREGORY BATESON

■ Goodbye and Good Luck to Margaret Mead and Gregory Bateson, *ink on paper drawing by I Ketoet Ngéndon of Batoean, 1938. The Balinese presented Mead and Bateson with this drawing on their departure to New Guinea. Mead and Bateson are in the ship. The Balinese are above, next to a volcano (as Mead described it) "belching forth 'Goodbye and Good Luck' in an elegant scroll design—and in English!" The Papuans are in the lower front of the picture, welcoming the pair.*

Mead enjoyed the Tambunam people immensely. Where the Balinese people had been even-tempered and steady in their everyday lives, saving their drama for their customs and theatrics, the Tambunam were the opposite. All day they fought good-naturedly and made noise. Mead and Bateson, meanwhile, devoted their efforts to making their field techniques uniform so they could be used universally by anthropologists. After six months, however, Mead and Bateson had to return; the war was coming. But there was another reason Mead was eager to get home: she was pregnant. Having already suffered many painful miscarriages, she was determined not to lose the baby.

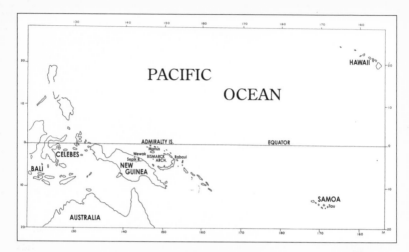

■ *This map of the South Pacific and Indonesia shows each of Mead's main fieldwork sites: Samoa (1925), the Admiralty Islands (1928), Papua New Guinea (1931), and Bali (1936). She studied several cultures in each region.*

MAP BY NICHOLAS AMOROSI

■ *Mead's fieldwork dress. Mead designed this dress to wear on location. Light cotton in case of extreme heat, it had a wraparound waist to accommodate weight loss and gain, and large pockets to hold notebooks.*

COURTESY THE SMITHSONIAN INSTITUTION,
NATIONAL MUSEUM OF AMERICAN HISTORY, BEHRING CENTER

FIELDWORK

AT TURNS INTENSE, frustrating, and rewarding, Mead's fieldwork was anything but easy. First she had to learn each language, a feat that, in the case of the Arapesh, meant sorting out "eleven genders and twenty-two third-person pronouns." Taking every opportunity to participate first-hand, Mead threw herself into the day-to-day living of the cultures she studied, engaging in activities like dyeing grass skirts and fishing. Throughout, she soaked in as much of the culture as possible. To do so, she also had to learn the accepted customs and taboos. In Bali, for example, "Anyone who visits a house where there is a new baby under 12 days old . . . becomes ceremonially unclean . . . until one has slept a full night in one's own house. (Note: Visit a new baby near the end of the day.)" And she had to be flexible in dealing with things like accommodations, food, and basic tasks: in Samoa, "When I bathed I had to learn to wear a sarong-like garment which I could slip off under the village shower as I slipped a dry one on in full view of the staring crowds of children and passing adults." She took detailed notes on everything she observed, from "the width of a basket" to "what you really do call your mother's brother."

The people Mead studied were generally tolerant of her presence and willing to talk with her, sometimes in exchange for gifts. Of the Arapesh, she wrote, "They like to have us here as a neighborhood store, as it were. It is convenient to be able to get salt and matches and knives and pipes and beads whenever they wish. They are quite willing to talk to us to keep us amused, as talk seems to be what we want." With her Western first-aid kit,

Mead often served as the village doctor, regularly dressing wounds and lowering fevers. Although ritual ceremonies surrounding major events like birth, death, and marriage provided the richest material, Mead got just as much out of passing simple time among her subjects. At night in Samoa, for example, "The young people bring their guitars and ukeleles and dance for me. A few new ones come every night. . . ."

While her fieldwork was productive, it could also be brutal, both mentally and physically. Although she often had malaria, each new attack of fever was "frightening because one gets so cold that it is hard to believe one will ever be warm again and stop shaking." Mosquitoes in the Sepik region were so bad that Mead wrote in a letter home, "Bathing except at midday has to be done with a whisk in one hand." Tangible results sometimes eluded her. "I feel as if I had no sense of values left, when I try to evaluate this work," she wrote Benedict from Omaha. Fieldwork, too, could be dangerous; other anthropologists had died in the field, and before each major trip, Mead updated her will. Before she and Bateson went back to the Sepik, she had her lawyer draw up a trust that would provide for the cataloging of their material from Bali in case anything happened to either of them.

Mead actively explored new field techniques like interviewing, using still and moving film, and collecting drawings from children, hoping to standardize these anthropological methods for future fieldworkers, who, thanks to her, would never have to feel the uncertainty she had felt in Samoa when she wrote, "The truth was that I had no idea whether I was using the right methods. . . . There were no precedents to fall back on." ■

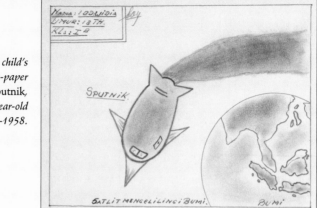

■ *Balinese child's pencil-on-paper drawing of Sputnik, by thirteen-year-old male, c. 1957–1958.*

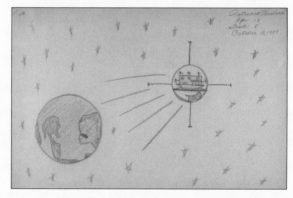

■ *American child's crayon-on-paper drawing of Sputnik, by thirteen-year-old female, 1957. Mead was fascinated with children's reactions to world events. Soon after Sputnik launched in 1957, Mead called her former student and friend Pat Grinager, who was teaching art in upstate New York, and asked her to collect students' artistic interpretations of the event. Later that year, Mead posed the same challenge to a group of Balinese students for comparison.*

A WARTIME UTOPIA

BACK IN NEW YORK, Mead busied herself getting ready for the baby. In her case, she needed more than cribs and bottles; she had to find a doctor who would support unconventional childbirth and child-rearing practices. She wanted her birth to be natural—no painkillers. She also wanted it to be filmed, which her daughter later called "a procedure that was almost unheard of in those days." And she wanted to breast-feed her baby whenever the child was hungry rather than on the fixed schedule that was routine at the time. Mead secured the services of Dr. Benjamin Spock, a pediatrician who later became famous for his own broad approach to child rearing.

Mead gave birth to a daughter, Mary Catherine Bateson, on December 8, 1939, naming her for Bateson's aunt and her own younger sister who died in infancy. If anybody thought a baby would slow Margaret Mead down, they were sorely mistaken. For Mead, motherhood and her career would coexist, just as they had for her mother and her grandmother before her. She and Bateson worked on cataloging the film they had taken in Bali, and Mead continued her busy schedule of lecturing, teaching, and working at the American Museum of Natural History. She also started on her next book, *And Keep Your Powder Dry,* in which she applied the analytic methods she had used on primitive, faraway cultures to contemporary American culture, an approach that amused some reviewers and riled others.

After the Japanese attacked Pearl Harbor in 1941, Larry Frank, who had organized the 1934 social science conference in Hanover, offered his home

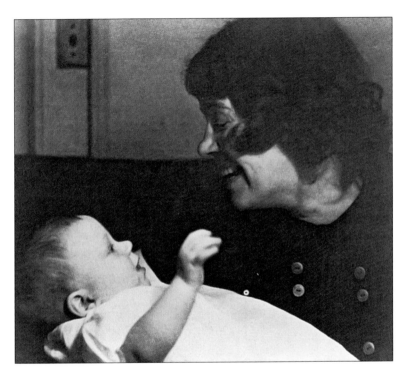

■ *Mead with her daughter, Mary Catherine Bateson, 1940. "I was completely happy,"*
Mead wrote of having her daughter. Although Mead was often away from Mary
Catherine, she made a large effort to spend quality time with her. Several times a week
she cooked dinner for her daughter, completed by one of her famous salads. Often, she
took Mary Catherine with her to the American Museum of Natural History and on trips.

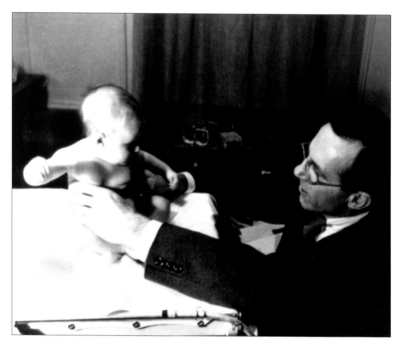

■ *Dr. Benjamin Spock examining Mary Catherine Bateson, c. 1940. A pediatrician with training in psychoanalysis, Spock became one of the best-selling authors of all time with his* Common Sense Book of Baby and Child Care, *in which he advocated flexibility in catering to each child's specific needs despite the prevailing belief in strictness and scheduling.*

■ *Social scientist Larry Frank, whose family shared their home with Mead's during the war. At the Franks', Mary Catherine grew up in a "large household organized for wartime."*

COURTESY THE NATIONAL LIBRARY OF MEDICINE

to Mead's family, an arrangement that would last until 1955. This "large household organized for wartime" also included Larry's five children from two previous marriages, his new wife and their infant son, and various visitors who passed through, some for extended periods of time. The brood lived in a large house in New York City and summered in New Hampshire. Mary Catherine fondly remembered these years as "utopia."

Between working and traveling, Mead often relied on the various members of this household to care for Mary Catherine, a task that fell usually to Larry's wife, Mary, and to Mead's good friends Marie Eichelberger (whom the children all called "Aunt Marie") and Sara Ullman, who lived down the street. Thus, Mary Catherine was influenced by a variety of adult figures and had numerous playmates, a situation that benefited her, allowed her mother to pursue her career without worrying about her daughter's physical care, and echoed the patriotic World War II sentiment of everyone pitching in.

In 1942, Mead and Bateson became members of the Committee on National Morale, a group of social scientists who discussed ways in which their fields could be applied to the world's current state. Mead's involvement reflected her growing interest in uniting the social sciences and using them to improve modern-day societies and ensure their peaceful coexistence.

That same year, Mead's old friend Ruth Benedict recruited her to be the executive secretary of the National Research Council's Committee on Food Habits, which studied the world's culture-specific dietary needs and determined the best ways for people to get the food they most wanted and needed. Mead procured a leave of absence from the museum and from Columbia University to take the job, which required her presence in Washington, DC. She commuted back to New York to be with her daughter on the weekends and maintained her usual vigorous schedule of public speaking appearances.

In 1944, Mead helped found the Institute of Intercultural Studies, an organization that supported the fieldwork of promising young anthropologists. It is still in existence today, now led by Mead's daughter. Mead also contributed to the war effort by teaching orientation courses to people going to the South Seas and by traveling, in the summer of 1943, to England at the behest of the Office of War Information to apply her expertise on courtship to the cultural problems arising from American boys dating English girls.

While Mead was in England, Bateson was in Washington, DC, and then sent on a twenty-month assignment to Asia to study psychological warfare. Their time apart took its toll on the marriage; Mead and Bateson no longer shared a common professional goal as they had in the field. The pair officially divorced in 1950. Her third divorce—the only one she had not initiated—was hard for Mead. She had loved Bateson in a way she had not loved her first two husbands. She would not marry again.

The end of Mead's marriage coincided with the end of the war. Mead wrote, "The atomic bomb exploded over Hiroshima in the summer of 1945. . . . We had entered a new age. My years as a collaborating wife, trying to combine intensive field work and an intense personal life, also came to an end. From that time on I worked not with one other person but with many others, as my child grew up secure within the generosities of the Frank household."

A CHANGED WORLD

MEAD REVISITED MANUS, the site of her 1928 fieldwork with Fortune, in 1953, after hearing about the massive changes that had occurred there as a result of the war. Now in her fifties, she threw herself into planning for her trip. She raised funds from the museum and the Rockefeller Foundation and searched for proper companions, whom she found in the form of a multitalented young anthropologist named Theodore Schwartz and his bright young wife, Lenora.

Mead found Manus, which had been a US army base during the war, much changed. The village, once raised above water on stilts, had been rebuilt on dry land. But the changes went much deeper than that; traditional customs were now basically nonexistent. The people of Pere had thrown out their dancing and magical curses and the dogs' teeth they used for money in favor of church and village meetings. Mead welcomed some of these changes and lamented others. She worried that present-day villagers would not be able to evolve into modern society, that they would be stuck halfway between the past and the present. The book that resulted from this research was *New Lives for the Old,* published in 1956. Mead found aspects of transitory culture so fascinating that in 1957 she returned to Bali,

■ *Mead with Lenora and Ted Schwartz and Manus children, 1953. Ted and Lenora were Mead's first fieldwork partners after the war; she spent six months training the couple on everything from administering psychological tests to avoiding extra-baggage charges at the airport.* PHOTOGRAPH BY THEODORE OR LENORA SCHWARTZ

■ *Mead's Manus houseboys as children, 1928. From left to right: Kapeli, Pomat, Yesa, Kilipak, and Loponiu. This original houseboy photograph, titled "Five Retainers," appeared in Mead's book* Growing Up in New Guinea *(1930). Mead revisited her houseboys twenty-five years later.* PHOTOGRAPH BY MARGARET MEAD

and in 1967, to the Tambunam peoples, whom she had studied with Bateson in 1938.

Mead continued her work at the American Museum of Natural History in New York. Although she was not made a full curator until 1964, the museum offered flexibility, a trait Mead cherished. There, she hired a number of assistants, launching the careers of many bright young scholars, mostly women. Pat Grinager, a student who volunteered in Mead's office and remained a lifelong friend, noted that "What she perceived as ineptitude

■ *Mead with her houseboys as adults, 1953. From left to right: Johanis Lokus (Loponiu),*
Mead, Petrus Pomat, Raphael Manuwai (not in 1928 photo), John Kilipak, and Manus
children. PHOTOGRAPH BY THEODORE OR LENORA SCHWARTZ

■ *Beginning in 1961, Mead wrote a monthly column in* Redbook *addressing a wide range of questions, including "When you were a little girl, who were your heroes and heroines in American history?" and "How do you feel about school boycotts as a way of solving school integration problems in Northern cities?"*

PHOTOGRAPH COURTESY
REDBOOK

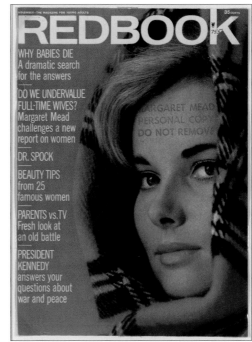

NOVEMBER · THE MAGAZINE FOR YOUNG ADULTS

REDBOOK

35 CENTS

WHY BABIES DIE
A dramatic search
for the answers

DO WE UNDERVALUE
FULL-TIME WIVES?
Margaret Mead
challenges a new
report on women

DR. SPOCK

BEAUTY TIPS
from 25
famous women

PARENTS vs. TV
Fresh look at
an old battle

PRESIDENT
KENNEDY
answers your
questions about
war and peace

MARGARET MEAD
PERSONAL COPY
DO NOT REMOVE

■ *Mead (right) with Rhoda Metraux, looking at American children's drawings of Sputnik, 1958. Mead met Metraux, a fellow anthropologist, during the war. The two friends lived together from 1955 until Mead's death.* PHOTOGRAPH BY ARTHUR HERZOG

or stupidity frequently frustrated her to the point of fury." Mead, though, was endlessly supportive of the assistants who withstood her tempers, offering recommendations and career advice long after they had left. Grinager, herself the recipient of connections through Mead, wrote that "Margaret Mead ran her own employment agency. . . . She . . . mixed and matched hundreds of jobs she heard about to people she considered could do them."

A major accomplishment was the 1971 opening of the Hall of the Peoples of the Pacific at the American Museum of Natural History, an endeavor she had seen through conception, planning, and construction. Mead contributed many of the artifacts in the permanent exhibit from her own collections.

As she aged, Mead continued to speak publicly on topics ranging from the generation gap to nuclear energy and ecological responsibility, quietly donating much of her speaking fees to anthropological research. She enjoyed attending conferences immensely, especially the annual meeting of the American Anthropology Association. Her presence at these conferences excited some and frightened others; according to Grinager, "When she disagreed with a remark . . . she stood by her seat, turned to face the

■ *Mead and an assistant in a storage room in her southwest tower office in the American Museum of Natural History, New York, 1960. Mead was originally assigned to this unusual "office," formerly a custodian's quarters, because of lack of space, but she chose to stay even after space opened up in the main part of the building. She said the office reminded her of when she moved into a new house as a girl and always picked a room "at the top of the house where I would always be warned by footsteps that someone was coming."* PHOTOGRAPH BY KEN HEYMAN

■ *Mead giving a telelecture at Omaha University, Omaha, Nebraska, November 11,*
1960. Mead was an avid guest speaker and lecturer, using new technology as it became
available to bring her ideas to a larger audience. During this lecture, a still image of her
appeared on a screen at the front of the room; she delivered the lecture via telephone,
which was projected into the room by a loudspeaker so the students could hear her
and vice versa.

audience in a room suddenly silenced and pounded her criticisms home with forked stick and tongue."

Mead also used her frequent travels as a way to visit her loved ones around the world—her siblings, cousins, former students, colleagues, and most importantly, her daughter—truly uniting her work and private life into one seamless whole.

For Mead's seventy-fifth birthday, the American Association for the Advancement of Science, a prestigious organization she had presided over for three years, held a large celebration, including tribute speeches from various colleagues. Numerous popular periodicals ran stories about Mead for the occasion, and she basked in the attention she had so rightfully earned. She was widely quoted to have said, "I expect to die, but I don't plan to retire."

Margaret Mead's for Legal Pot

Washington, Oct. 27 (UPI) —Anthropologist Margaret Mead told senators today that marijuana should be legalized for anyone over 16 and that drinking and voting ages should match the draft age.

Prof. Mead, 67, said the harsh laws against marijuana use are damaging society much more than the prohibition on liquor in the 1920s and are forcing youngsters to turn to hard drugs such as heroin.

"A New Form of Tyranny"

She did not mention a minimum age for marijuana use in her testimony before Sen. Gaylord Nelson's Senate Small Business Monopoly subcommittee. But she told newsmen afterward that the minimum age should be "probably 16."

She said marijuana "doesn't have the toxic effects that cigarets have" and is milder than liquor. Therefore, she said, it should be permitted at a younger age than tobacco and alcohol.

Prof. Mead told the senators: "It is a new form of tyranny by the old over the young. You have the adult with a cocktail in one hand and a cigaret in the other saying: 'You cannot. . .' to the child. This is untenable."

Book About the Gap

She said youngsters s w i t c h from marijuana to hard drugs because of a philosophy that "you might as well be hung as a sheep as a lamb."

Prof. Mead, who recently wrote a book about the generation gap,

Anthropologist Margaret Mead testifying on use of marijuana.

told the senators that medical evidence l e a v e s no doubt that marijuana is not addictive, does not by itself lead the user to hard drugs and is much milder in its effects than alcohol.

She said 99% of marijuana smokers never switch to harder drugs. Those who do, she said,

are probably motivated by the harsh laws.

Prof. Mead is curator emeritus of ethnology at the American Museum of Natural History and professor of anthropology at Columbia University. She gained fame for her studies of natives in Samoa and New Guinea.

MEAD AND THE CRITICS

LIKE ANY PUBLIC FIGURE, Mead was not without her critics. In a letter to a colleague, she once wrote, "I have got accustomed to being treated as anthropologically non-existent." Indeed, she was often an outsider in the field of anthropology. Some of her colleagues disdained her for "dumbing down" anthropology by writing to a popular audience rather than a scholarly one. She was also criticized for her decision to live with a white family in Samoa, and some questioned whether she really could have learned the Samoan language in just six short weeks.

Her most vocal critic was a New Zealand–born Australian anthropologist named Derek Freeman. Freeman's book *Margaret Mead and Samoa*, published in 1983, five years after Mead's death, asserted that her research was wrong and that Samoan adolescence and culture were more complicated than she had made it seem. Further, he accused Mead of tailoring her research to prove her—

■ *"Margaret Mead's for Legal Pot," United Press International article, Washington, DC, October 27, 1969. Mead's often unconventional views earned her many critics. This article, written after Mead stood before Congress to speak for the legalization of marijuana, was sent to her by an angry citizen, complete with handwritten notes in the margin. Mead wrote that she had come to terms with "the way in which I have been publicly discussed, lambasted and lampooned, lionized and mythologized, called an institution and a stormy petrel, and cartooned as a candidate for the Presidency, wearing a human skull around my neck as an ornament. I have taken the stand, in my own mind and replying to others, that I have no right to resent the public expression of attitudes that I arouse in those whom I do not know and who know me only through what I have written or said and through the words that the mass media, correctly or incorrectly, have contributed to me."* PHOTOGRAPH COURTESY UPI

and Boas'—preconceived notions of nature versus nurture. He based his conclusions on his six cumulative years of research in Samoa, beginning in 1940.

Freeman's assertions erupted into an international scandal, ranging from the United States to Samoa to Australia. Mead's supporters were angry that Freeman was publishing his book when Mead was no longer alive to defend herself. They also pointed out that Freeman's book in 1983 depicted a much different Samoa than the one Mead had studied in 1925, and that most of his research had been done more than one hundred miles west of Mead's field site.

Freeman went head to head with Mary Catherine Bateson, herself now an accomplished anthropologist, on the *CBS Morning News* and *The Phil Donahue Show*. Bradd Shore, another anthropologist with expertise on Samoa, also appeared on the Donahue show and explained, "Margaret Mead was not completely wrong on Samoa. . . . She was incomplete. And when someone is incomplete you don't refute them, you correct, you add, and you also acknowledge what you have learned from them. . . ." "That," Bateson added, "is called science." ■

■ *Mead's daughter, Mary Catherine Bateson, followed her parents into the field of anthropology. She wrote that "The complex mosaic of friendships in which we moved provided as vivid an introduction to anthropology as any field trip would have."*
PHOTOGRAPH BY FRED ROLL

"Young men, you've now reached the age when it is essential that you know the rites and rituals, the customs and taboos of our island. Rather than go into them in detail, however, I'm simply going to present each of you with a copy of this excellent book by Margaret Mead."

Drawing by Alain
Copyright 1956 The New Yorker Magazine, Inc.

■ *Cartoon in the New Yorker, 1956. Mead was the subject of many cartoons. This one, by Alain (Daniel Brustlein), pokes fun at the overwhelming success of* Coming of Age in Samoa, *asserting that elder Samoans need not bother teaching their youth Samoan customs that are so readily found in Mead's book.*

■ *John Kilipak of New Guinea presenting a money belt to the American Museum of Natural History, 1979. Catherine Bateson (right), her daughter Vanni (middle), and Rhoda Metraux (left) accept the gift to the museum. Kilipak was a subject of Mead's 1928 field research in Manus, when he was thirteen years old.*

PHOTOGRAPH BY PETER GOLDBERG

EPILOGUE

MEAD NEVER DID RETIRE. She died of pancreatic cancer on November 15, 1978. She maintained her busy schedule until the last few weeks of her illness, traveling all over the world, meeting young scholars, and giving speeches. She did not want to admit that she was sick to her friends and, most of all, to herself. She had too much planned and too much to do.

On hearing of her death, the village of Pere in Manus declared a week-long mourning period. The village councilman sent a telegram that read, "People sorry of Margaret Mead's death—with sympathy, respect. Rested seven days. Planted coconut tree memory of great friend." The memorials at home were of equal sentiment. A large funeral was held at the National Cathedral in Washington, DC, in December. The following month, the American Museum of Natural History—where Mead had worked for more than fifty years—held a memorial service, at which the Presidential Medal of Freedom was presented to her daughter. A park on the museum's grounds was named Margaret Mead Green in her honor.

Called "a genius of the prophetic sort" by one reviewer, Mead left behind an enormous body of work. She wrote or collaborated on almost forty books, penned over a thousand articles for both scholarly publications and popular periodicals, and created more than forty records, films, and tape recordings. She was survived by a vast number of people whose lives she had touched—family, friends, colleagues, former students, and countless others—but the effect she had on people she never met was just as profound. She felt her most significant contribution was "to introduce anthropology to the general, literate public." As she had always hoped, Mead made a name for herself, daring to pioneer an emerging discipline and secure her place in history. But more importantly, she made a name for a field she passionately believed could improve people's lives, describing anthropology as "the attempt to understand enough about culture so that all of us, equally members of humankind, can understand ourselves and take our future and the future of our descendants safely in our hands." ■

■ *Mead in Hancock, New Hampshire, May 26, 1975. After the third and last time Mead broke her ankle, in 1960, she bought a forked walking stick to use as her ankle healed. She continued to use the stick even after she no longer needed it, because she liked the aura it gave her. The forked stick—along with the capes she favored in later life— became part of her public image.* PHOTOGRAPH BY SHARI SEGEL

FURTHER READING AND SOURCES

Margaret Mead's papers are housed in the Manuscript Division of the Library of Congress. The collection holds over five hundred thousand items, including correspondence, field notes, and photographs.

Bateson, Mary Catherine. *With a Daughter's Eye: A Memoir of Margaret Mead and Gregory Bateson*. New York: Harper, Perennial, 2001. First published 1984 by William Morrow.

Bowman-Kruhm, Mary. *Margaret Mead: A Biography*. Westport, CT: Greenwood Press, 2003.

Cressman, Luther. *A Golden Journey: Memoirs of an Archaeologist*. Salt Lake City: University of Utah Press, 1988.

Grinager, Patricia. *Uncommon Lives: My Lifelong Friendship with Margaret Mead*. Lanham, MD: Rowman & Littlefield, 1999.

Howard, Jane. *Margaret Mead: A Life*. New York: Simon & Schuster, 1984.

Mead, Margaret. *Blackberry Winter: My Earlier Years*. New York: William Morrow, 1972.

———. *Coming of Age in Samoa: A Psychological Study of Primitive Youth for Western Civilisation*. New York: Harper, Perennial, 2001. First published 1928 by William Morrow.

———. *Letters from the Field, 1925–1975*. New York: Harper & Row, 1977.

Metraux, Rhoda, ed. *Margaret Mead: Some Personal Views*. New York: Walker, 1979.

Ziesk, Edra. *Margaret Mead*. New York: Chelsea House, 1990.

ACKNOWLEDGMENTS

The author wishes to thank Amy Pastan, series editor, for her ideas and hard work. She is also grateful to Janice Ruth of the Mead Papers in the Manuscript Division at the Library of Congress for her help in obtaining images for this book, and to Ann Brownell Sloane, Executive Director, and Betty Howe, Permissions Assistant, at the Institute for Intercultural Studies for permission to use them. Many thanks to Mary Catherine Bateson for her cooperation and assistance.

IMAGES

Unless otherwise noted, images are from the Margaret Mead Collection in the Manuscript Division of the Library of Congress. Reproduction numbers are given when available. To order reproductions, note the LC- number provided with the image; where no number exists, note the Library division and the title of the item. Direct your request to:

The Library of Congress
Photoduplication Service
Washington DC 20540-4570
(202) 707-5640; www.loc.gov